On Your Plate

Salad
Honor Head

A⁺

Smart Apple Media

Smart Apple Media
P.O. Box 3263, Mankato, Minnesota 56002

RAP 8619126

Printed in the United States

Published by arrangement with the Watts Publishing Group Ltd, London.

Created by Taglines
Design: Sumit Charles; Harleen Mehta, Q2A Media
Picture research: Pritika Ghura, Q2A Media

Picture credits
t=top b=bottom c=center l=left r=right m=middle
Cover Images: Shutterstock, Istock and Dreamstime.
Q2A Media: 4b, 17br, Heather Lewis/ Shutterstock: 5t, Anton Gvozdikov/ Shutterstock: 5b, Jacek Chabraszewski/ Shutterstock:
6b, PhantomOfTheOpera/ Istockphoto: 7b, rj lerich/ Shutterstock: 8bl, 15, Og-vision | Dreamstime.com: 8bm, Marc Dietrich/
Shutterstock: 8br, Juriah Mosin/ Shutterstock: 9, Joe Gough/ Istockphoto: 11bl, Alex Balako/ Shutterstock: 11br, Isatori |
Dreamstime.com: 12, Antonio Jorge Nunes/ Shutterstock: 13, Joss | Dreamstime.com: 14, khwi/ Shutterstock: 16, Andriy
Doriy/ Shutterstock: 17bl, Danny Smythe/ Shutterstock: 18, Clay Clifford/ Shutterstock: 19, Leon Forado/ Shutterstock: 20,
Paul Schneider/ Shutterstock: 21, Roman Sigaev/ Shutterstock: 22.

Library of Congress Cataloging-in-Publication Data

Head, Honor.
  Salad / Honor Head.
      p. cm. -- (On your plate)
  Includes index.
  Summary: "Provides basic introductions to what foods go into a salad, different kinds of salads, and why they are good to
eat."--Provided by publisher.
  ISBN 978-1-59920-259-4
  1. Salads--Juvenile literature. 2. Salad vegetables--Juvenile literature. I. Title.
  TX807.H373 2010
  641.8'3--dc22
                                                                                                                    2008039931

9 8 7 6 5 4 3 2 1

Contents

What is salad?

A salad is a mix of vegetables or fruit. We usually eat salads cold.

  Salads taste good with different dressings on them.

Cherry tomatoes can be eaten whole in a salad.

You can cut up bigger tomatoes and add them to a salad.

Cucumbers

Cucumbers have a green skin.
You can eat the skin.

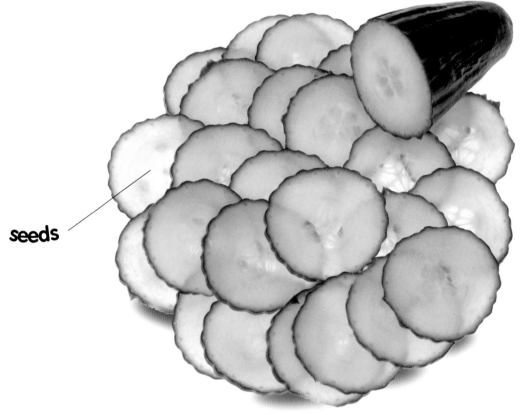

seeds

There are tiny seeds inside a cucumber.

Pickles can be chopped into a salad for extra flavor.

Pickles are young cucumbers. They are pickled in vinegar.

Green Salad

A green salad is a mix of lettuce and other green leaves.

iceberg lettuce

romaine lettuce

round lettuce

8

 Lettuce can stay fresh for up to three weeks.

You can eat a green salad as a meal or as a side dish with your main meal.

Add cherry tomatoes and cucumbers to a green salad for a filling lunch.

Onions

Green onions are onions that are picked before they are fully grown.

 Try some green onions chopped in your salad.

Red onions taste sweeter than other onions. Red onion rings are eaten raw in salads.

 Red onions add color and taste to a salad.

11

Beets

Beets are cooked before they are eaten cold.

Beets grow in the ground.

Beet juice has a strong red color.

beets

Eating beets helps you quickly get over a cold or illness.

Peppers

You can buy green, red, orange, and yellow peppers.

  The white seeds inside a pepper are thrown away.

Peppers can be fried and put on meat, or eaten raw with dip.

 Slices of pepper make a crunchy side dish.

Corn

When corn is picked, it is covered by a husk. Inside are the corn kernels.

husk

kernel

Corn like this is called corn on the cob.

Corn kernels are sold in cans.
You can sprinkle them on salads.

Corn kernels are
sometimes called
niblets.

Mushrooms

Mushrooms grow in damp places. Fresh mushrooms are eaten raw in salads.

 Big mushrooms have a strong flavor.

Before you eat mushrooms, always wash away any dirt you can see on them.

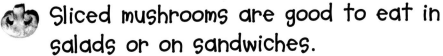 Sliced mushrooms are good to eat in salads or on sandwiches.

19

Celery

Long stalks of celery grow in bunches above the ground.

Most people eat the pale celery stalks. They do not eat the green leaves.

Munching on celery helps your teeth and gums stay strong.

Try crunchy sticks of celery with peanut butter.

21

Things to Do

Salad Bowl Puzzle

Can you recognize what is in this salad bowl?

Oh No!

This salad has been covered in beet juice.
What color should the vegetables be?

Salad Selection

Can you guess what is in this salad from these descriptions?

a)   I am long and green with small seeds inside.

b)   I am red and juicy.

c)   I am crunchy and have green leaves.

23

Glossary

husk
The covering on the outside of corn when it is growing.

pickle
To food into vinegar to make it last a long time.

seeds
The part of a plant that new plants grow from.

stalk
The long, stiff part of a plant where the leaves and flowers grow.

Index